DADS ARE SPECIAL, TOO

DADS ARE SPECIAL, TOO

JOHN DAVID PURDY

TYNDALE HOUSE
PUBLISHERS, INC.
WHEATON, ILLINOIS

ACKNOWLEDGMENTS
My thanks to Foster Cline, Charles Downing, Jean Foster, Dianne Key, Kristofa Otabi, Mary Regan, Terry Truffin, and Bob and Dorothy Purdy for their encouragement and contributions.

The following publishers have generously given permission to use extended quotations from copyrighted works: From *Hide or Seek,* by James Dobson, Ph.D. Copyright 1974, 1979 by Fleming H. Revell Company. Used by permission of the publisher, Fleming H. Revell Company. From *The Hurried Child,* by David Elkind. Copyright 1981 by David Elkind. Used by permission of the publisher, Addison-Wesley Publishing Company. From *Christian Child-Rearing and Personality Development,* by Paul D. Meier. Copyright 1977 by Baker Book House. Used by permission of the publisher, Baker Book House.

First printing, May 1985
Library of Congress Catalog Card Number 85-50029
ISBN 0-8423-0503-3, paper

Printed in the United States of America

This book is dedicated
to my family—
God's personal blessing to me—
my wife, Ann,
and our children,
Benjamin, Hannah, and Carolyn.

CONTENTS

FOREWORD

Parenting—it can be so tough or so easy. Children can detract from our lives or add to them immeasurably.

What is the prerequisite for becoming a parent? In the work world, most of us look askance at receiving only on-the-job training. Even McDonald's considers it tacky to turn out french fries without training the cook. Training is required to work in the average garage and the public library. But there is no training required to become a parent!

Worse yet, these kids come without an instruction manual. Operating over the years by guess and by golly, many a parent raises a child that he himself wouldn't want to pick up off the shelf as an adolescent. In my private practice, I realize only too well that all the mistakes a loving parent may make when the child is young are repaid in triplicate when the child reaches high school.

So I'm very excited about good instruction manuals on raising children. This is one of them.

With clear examples and concise thoughts, David

Purdy explains the insights he has acquired through years of counseling and teaching parents. This book glows with his warmth, personality, and wisdom.

It is a pleasure to read the wisdom of a person who lives it. When David is with his children, he exemplifies meaning business without being mean. And when he means business, he comes across as firm, not angry.

In summary, this is a book to read and reread, to give as a present, to be underlined, scribbled in, and used often. In fact, I can safely say that the more this book becomes well-worn, the less you as parents will be!

Foster W. Cline, M.D.
Child Psychiatrist
Director of Evergreen Consultants
in Human Behavior

INTRODUCTION

We have a plaque in our bedroom that reads, "Anyone can be a Father, but it takes someone special to be a Daddy." This is an interesting and compelling thought, but what exactly makes a daddy *special?*

I don't intend to convey the notion that a Special Dad is some kind of bionic Superdad endowed with extraterrestrial powers. Special Dads don't ride around on white horses or spend every waking hour studying child growth and development journals. Special Dads get frustrated, upset, and sometimes lose their temper. They even may feel certain inadequacies as they relate to their children.

Nevertheless, in the eyes of most every child, Daddy is special simply because he is Daddy. In essence, all Daddies are special, but many of us don't know it. Teachers have substitutes and presidents have successors, but, Dad, you are irreplaceable. You are a special person with the privilege and opportunity to influence your children in a unique and wonderful way.

The Lamaze childbirth courses are excellent. They foster communication between a husband and a wife, enabling men to become more intimately involved in the birth process.

And yet, what do we do when our little ones come home from the hospital? We tend to assume our fathering roles in the same way our own fathers did. For example, those unfortunate enough to have been abused as children often become child abusers as adults. Conversely, we may go toward the other extreme of behavior. "I'm going to see to it my kids have all the things in life I never had," we say. Then we proceed to spoil and indulge them.

Other than using our own parents as role models, we normally learn to care for our children by on-the-job training. Can you imagine going into the working world with as little experience?

Admittedly, with or without experience, being a father is not always smooth sailing. As I walked down the boardwalk at Ocean City, Maryland, a few years ago, a rather haggard-looking couple trudged toward me with an armload of beach supplies and three small children in tow. Everyone was obviously tired after a long day at the ocean. The children whined as they dragged along, clutching at their parents' T-shirts which quite fittingly read, "Insanity is inherited . . . you get it from your children."

One of the challenges we face as parents is just trying to understand these youngsters. In Art Linkletter's book of yesteryear, *Kids Say the Darndest Things,* are some humorous examples of children's reasoning and expression. In our own home we have encountered firsthand some entertaining, and sometimes surprising, incidents.

One afternoon my wife was tucking our reluctant two-year-old in for her nap. "I don't like myself," Carolyn sobbed, "because I have to take naps." "When Ben and Hannah were little, Mommy made them take naps, too," Mom consoled. With obvious relief, the enlightened Carolyn concluded thoughtfully, "I like myself, Mommy." After a moment's pause, she added triumphantly, "I don't like you!"

In the midst of our daily routine, it's so important to step back occasionally and, in clearer perspective, think in terms of long-range goals for our children. Most parents desire their children to become happy, well-adjusted young men and women, capable of making wise decisions and leading fruitful lives.

It is not uncommon, however, for these same well-meaning parents to inadvertently hinder the progess of their children. In many instances, the child's positive development depends upon the parents' willingness to change their own perspective and approach in relating to their children.

I recall a counseling session with the young father of a six-year-old. He was totally frustrated by his son's immaturity and lack of responsibility.

As we delved deeper into the family's interactions, it became apparent that the son was assuming the role he felt was expected of him. Dad was doing many things his son could and should have been doing for himself. He brushed his son's teeth, laid out his clothes, and made his bed.

The son was irresponsible because he never had been given the opportunity to become responsible. The poor fellow was made to feel totally dependent upon his father. This immature little boy was simply a product of his environment.

In order for this youngster to change, it was essential that his dad change, and change is not always easy. When confronted with the need to make certain adaptations, many are apt to respond, "Hey, this just isn't me" or, "That's not my style."

However, remember that walking was not your style at one point in your life. It was an awkward and sometimes frustrating experience. It was, nonetheless, necessary—unless you relish the thought of scrambling through life on your hands and knees.

A wise old coaching adage states, "The will to win is not nearly as important as the will to prepare to win." Winning doesn't just happen to us; neither does becoming an effective Special Daddy.

It is important for fathers to take an active role in parenting. Since women are frequently home more often than men, it is easy to subconsciously lay our responsibilities in Mother's lap. But effective fathering is not just doing what comes naturally. It is a real commitment, a labor of love.

This little book, although not intended as a complete study on parenting, might be a helpful guide. As you read, study, and implement the following ideas, it is my fervent hope that your experience as a father will become the rich and fulfilling adventure it is meant to be.

ONE

The Balanced Approach

WHEN I served as a high school counselor, I was often impressed by the vastly different attitudes, values, and life-styles of the students. I was especially impressed by those students who, although not the brightest, most popular, best-looking, or most athletic, were basically very well-adjusted. I saw in these students some of the traits I desired for my own children.

Consequently, I often asked the parents of these students their "secrets" to shaping these young lives so beautifully. I realize there are many factors outside of parenting that determine the uniqueness of each person, including genetics. But I am more inclined to feel that the temperament, disposition, and outlook of our children are to a large degree the result of our association with them as parents.

So I asked and discussed and found with uncanny regularity the same three responses echoed time and again: respect, love, and discipline. Although they are interrelated, each one is highly significant in itself.

much like the scale of justice, indicates the tremendous need for balance between these qualities. The two hands represent certain factors that can tip the scale and interfere with the healthy growth of our children: neglect and abuse, on the extreme side of discipline, and indulgence and pampering, on the extreme side of love.

BUILDING A CHILD:
THE BALANCED APPROACH

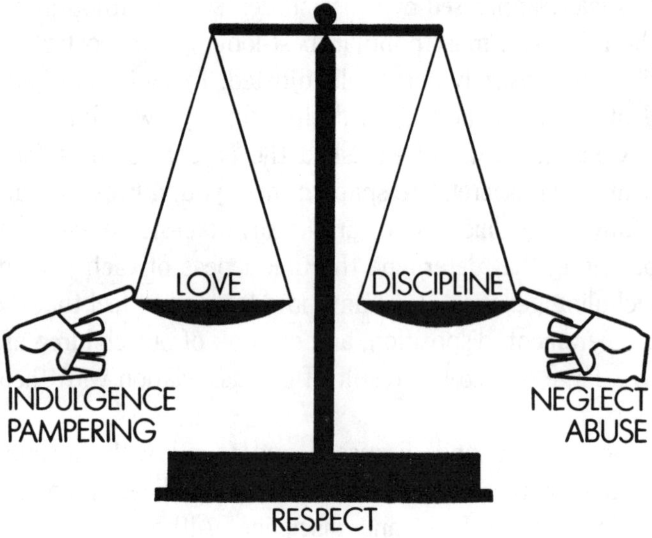

Some Dads and Moms mistakenly try to achieve the balanced approach by individually representing discipline and love. That is, the mother may feel that her husband is too strict. Therefore, she overcompensates and indulges the child. The father, determined his wife will not make a sissy out of his son, becomes more harsh. This rendition of a balanced approach is better likened to a vicious cycle. The balanced approach is best accomplished when the balance is achieved within each parent.

THE RESULTS OF IMBALANCE

The results of heavy-handedness at either end of the spectrum can produce discouraged children. A *dis*couraged child is one who has lost the *courage* to approach life in a positive and meaningful way. He doesn't feel he can live up to your or his own expectations. His feelings of insecurity cause him to seek out relationships where he is dominant or is being dominated. Feelings of equality are nonexistent, and his very self-centeredness leaves no time or regard for others.

Indeed, a discouraged child can be likened to a man who is drowning in a lake. He is so preoccupied with his present dilemma, he doesn't see the hands outstretched to save him. Furthermore, he doesn't view himself as a worthwhile person or as a contributing member of his family.

For the pampered child, attention becomes his life's goal. He wants immediate gratification and expects that others are positioned in life to serve him. Through his weakness he controls and manipulates them. New situa-

environment, tends to gravitate toward similar patterns of delinquency and depression. His feelings of rejection stimulate an attitude that says, "The only way to get things is to take them." He, too, uses and manipulates people for his own purposes. In effect, he cannot maintain positive relationships involving cooperation.

THE HELPLESS CHILD VS. THE HURRIED CHILD

An imbalanced approach to parenting can also hinder or hurry a child's social and emotional development.

The helpless child, who has been pampered, never learns to take care of himself because some adult is always there to watch over him. He doesn't have to pick up his socks because Mom will do it. He doesn't have to remember his library books because Dad will remind him. He believes that everything from his teeth to his toys is someone else's responsibility. As this youngster grows up, he will look for a spouse who will follow him around to pick up his socks and remind him of the time.

Some authorities term this behavior "learned helplessness." One of our parental responsibilities is to avoid this very common dilemma by teaching each child the value of self-reliance. James Dobson addresses this subject in his book, *Hide or Seek* (Revell, 1979).

> It is probably easier to foster an unhealthy dependency relationship between parent and child than it

> is to avoid one. The best preparation for responsible adulthood is derived from training in responsibility during childhood. This is not to say that a child is horsewhipped into acting like an adult. It does mean that the child be encouraged to progress on an orderly timetable of events, carrying the level of responsibility that is appropriate for his age.

Conversely, a growing number of children in the United States are growing up too fast, too soon. The Congressional Caucus for Women's Issues estimates as many as six million children care for themselves after school before their parents return home from work. These latch-key children, as they have been called, are among those who are unable to enjoy the innocence and joys of childhood because of neglect or other parental and societal pressures. David Elkind in his book, *The Hurried Child* (Addison-Wesley, 1981), explains:

> Unlike the spoiled children who remain children too long, hurried children grow up too fast. Hurried children are forced to take on the physical, psychological, and social trappings of adulthood before they are prepared to deal with them. We dress our children in miniature adult costumes (often with designer labels), we expose them to gratuitous sex and violence, and we expect them to cope with an increasingly bewildering social environment—divorce, single parenthood, homosexuality. Hurried children seem to make up a large portion of the troubled children seen by clinicians today; they constitute

We are faced with the task of providing a balanced environment for our children. Through our life-styles, values, and influences we are sending them some very important messages. The challenge for you, Dad, is to enable your youngster to progress responsibly without stressing his emotional equipment.

SECRETS OF A MODEL HOME

The results of an interesting study by a leading university were recently released. The study involved the type of home *least* likely to produce a juvenile delinquent. These model homes had four basic qualities in common: a father's discipline, a mother's supervision, an open display of affection in the home, and family cohesiveness.

Paul D. Meier, M.D., lists in his book, *Christian Child Rearing and Personality Development* (Baker, 1977), five characteristics of mentally healthy families:

a. *Love*—Parents should have genuine love for each other and for their children.
b. *Discipline*—A concept unpopular before the student activism of the "60's" is now coming back in vogue.
c. *Consistency*—Both parents should stick together, using the same rules and consistently enforcing those rules so that what a child gets away with on some occasions is not the cause for

which he is capriciously punished at another time.

d. *Example*—In healthy families, the parents don't expect the children to live up to standards they themselves don't keep. Parents should expect their children to live up to the standards they themselves observe.

e. *A man at the head of the home*—The vast majority of neurotics, both children and adults, grew up in homes where there was no father or the father was absent or weak, and the mother was domineering.

In *Hide or Seek*, James Dobson discusses a study made by Stanley Coopersmith, associate professor of psychology at the University of California.

> Dr. Coopersmith studied 1,738 normal middle-class boys and their families, beginning in the preadolescent period and following them through to young manhood. After identifying those boys having the highest self-esteem, he compared their homes and childhood influences with those having a lower sense of self-worth. He found three important characteristics which distinguished them: (1) The high-esteem children were clearly more loved and appreciated at home than were the low-esteem boys. . . . (2) The high-esteem group came from homes where parents had been significantly more strict in their approach to discipline. By contrast, the parents of the low-esteem group had created insecurity and

independent young men during the latter period of the study were found to have come from homes that demanded the strictest accountability and responsibility. And as could have been predicted, the family ties remained the strongest—not in the wishy-washy homes—but in the homes where discipline and self-control had been a way of life. (3) The homes of the high-esteem group were also characterized by democracy and openness. Once the boundaries for behavior were established, there was freedom for individual personalities to grow and develop. The boys could express themselves without fear of ridicule, and the overall atmosphere was marked by acceptance and emotional safety.

These various studies very much confirm the reports of the high school parents I questioned. In fact, the similarities are remarkable. Imagine how much time and effort we could have saved those scholars if only they had asked us!

Our early childhood experiences and how we interpret them are determinants of our life-styles as adults. That is why our relationships with our young children are so vital. This is not to say that we have total control over how each child will turn out. Certainly not. Yet the way we relate to our children directly influences their perceptions, conceptions, and misconceptions about life, people, and their personal role and function in society. Without a foundation of respect, love, and discipline, all other techniques and approaches to fathering lose significance.

TAKING STOCK: THE BALANCED APPROACH

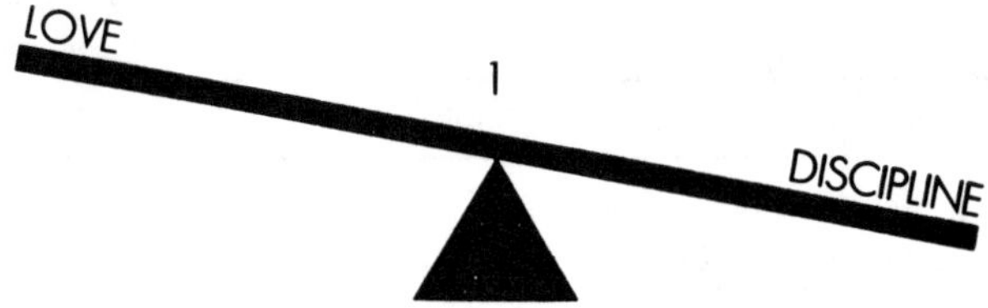

The kids are under control,
but there is not much warmth or love in our home.

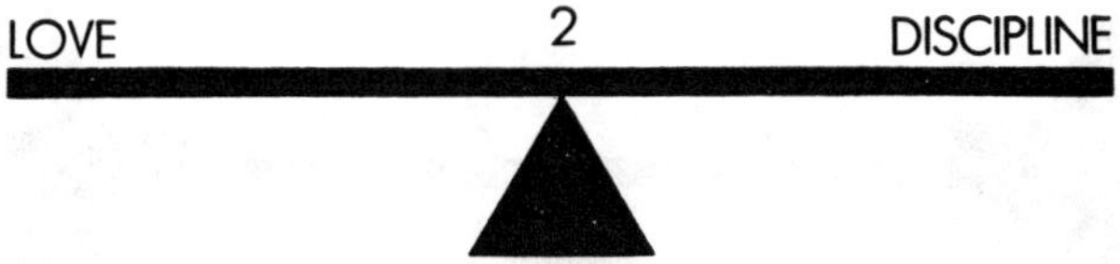

There is a lot of love in our home,
and the kids are under control.

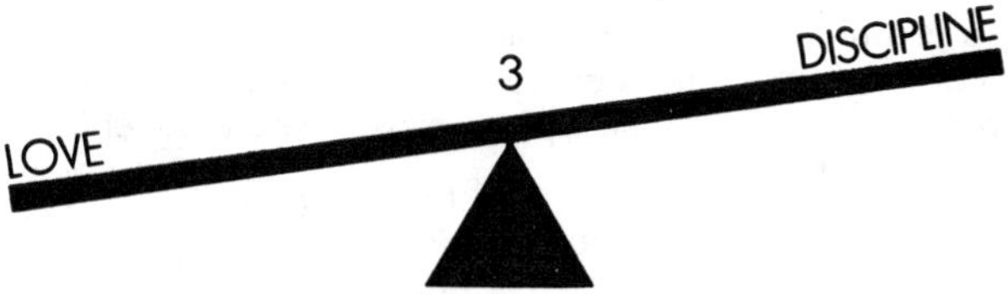

There is a lot of love in our home,
but the kids are out of control much of the time.

Which of these illustrations best describes your home?

Dad's response: ______________________________

____

Children's response: ____________________

____

____

THE HELPLESS CHILD

THE HURRIED CHILD

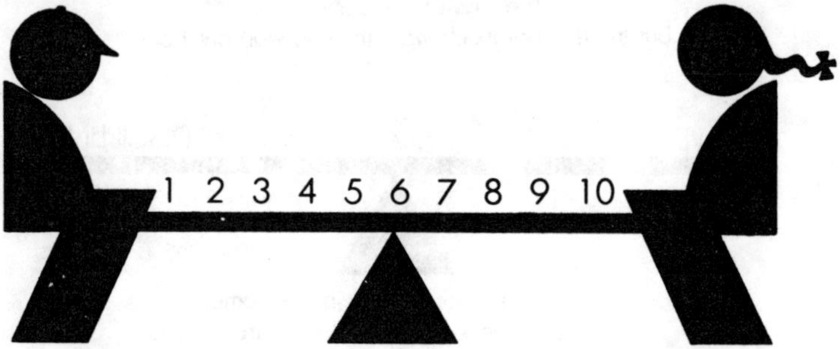

Seven-year-old Tony is growing up with the notion that everyone in life is here to serve him. His parents continually do for him, remember for him, make excuses for him. He is babied throughout his growing-up years.

On a scale of one to ten, which number best depicts your child?

Do you tend to influence your child to either extreme?

Seven-year-old Tina is a latch-key child. She spends countless unsupervised hours at home with full-time babysitting responsibilities. She wears makeup, reads teenage magazines, watches unlimited cable television, and is worldly beyond her years.

Take time to discuss your responses in a positive and constructive way with other members of your family. As you read through the remainder of the book, look for specific ways to maintain your balance or improve it. You may want to turn back to this page from time to time and write down additional thoughts and ideas.

TWO

Respect: Kids Need It, Too

SOME folks mistakenly equate love and respect. While they are similar qualities, they aren't exactly one and the same. Some children are assured that their parents love them, but there is a noticeable absence of respect in that love.

A good illustration of this is the incident involving the irresponsible six-year-old. Without a doubt, this father loved his son very much. However, it was quite evident that he was unaware of his son's needs to become more independent. Dad was assuming that his son was not capable of brushing his own teeth or making his bed. As adults, if others consider us incapable, we call it disrespect!

Respect should permeate both love and discipline. That is, our love needs to reflect the respect we hold for our children. Our disciplinary procedures likewise should be carried through in a manner that communicates our respect.

beings, but as smaller, younger people.

Although I advocate strong parental leadership, especially in the formative years, I believe it needs to be accompanied by sensitivity to the child's need for respect. Disrespect leads to low self-esteem. In turn, low self-esteem results in lost potential, underachievement, and general unhappiness. These are the exact opposites of the qualities most parents generally note in their long-range goals for their children.

Thus, respect is an attitude and perspective that assumes that children, although different from their parents in their role and level of authority, are equal to them in terms of their worth. It means that my children are equal to the neighbor's kids, the neighbors, other adults, and myself.

WATCH THOSE LABELS!

Respect includes avoiding comparisons between your child and other children. If my daughter has brown eyes and I comment on your daughter's beautiful blue eyes, adding that I am partial to blue eyes, what's my little girl going to assume? And she can't do anything about it.

This principle applies to physical appearance, development, school achievement, athletic ability, and even personality. If, in the presence of my children, I label my daughter as being the neat one in the family and my son the mess, not only will it hurt him deeply, but it will continue to reinforce what he already believes to be true. "I'm Jason, the walking pig pen. That's what's expected of me, and that's how I'll behave."

There will be enough comparisons without our contributions! One morning Hannah was trying to keep up with Benny in front-lawn gymnastics. He was jumping over an elevated broomstick, and in her attempts she was forever knocking it down. Finally, this little exasperated two-year-old exclaimed in dismay, "I can't do it, Ben. I'm not a boy, I'm a girl!"

We had never consciously made much reference to distinctions between male and female. But to our surprise, she had. She hadn't considered that her brother was two years older than she was. In her mind, the obvious reason for his success and her failure was a boy-girl difference.

Each child is unique and special, not because of what he does, but because of who he is. Yet in building up our youngsters, it is important to assist them in finding areas of compensation; that is, certain activities they particularly enjoy and excel in. For instance, an older son might be a particularly good athlete. A younger son might not be blessed in this area and may need to seek out other strengths, such as art, music, or mechanics. Identifying and pursuing areas of strength is beneficial in building self-confidence and self-esteem.

FOLLOW THE TIMETABLE

There are two basic types of maturity. Developmental or physiological maturity, in which children grow through orderly and predictable stages, is governed by the pitu-

Children will naturally proceed through various stages of social and emotional growth, but a caring adult has a great deal of influence on the outcome. For example, most children beginning at about eighteen months of age will exhibit some form of temper outbursts. But the severity and duration of these tantrums is often determined by parental response.

The table in this chapter highlights the basic differences between these two types of maturity. This book deals primarily with social and emotional development and how we, as fathers, can effectively influence these kinds of behavior. However, our response to the physiological development of our children is also important.

TYPES OF MATURITY

PHYSIOLOGICAL	SOCIAL/EMOTIONAL
Growth is determined by the pituitary gland.	Growth is based upon learned experiences.
Growth is orderly and predictable.	Growth varies from child to child based largely upon parent/child relationships.
Children will naturally outgrow these stages.	Children will *not* necessarily outgrow these stages.
Growth is *not* influenced by adult intervention.	Appropriate adjustment *is* influenced by adult intervention.
Examples: physical growth, visual perception, motor coordination.	Examples: self-control, sensitivity to others, self-esteem.

Please be sensitive to the fact that each child has his own timetable for development. Unfortunately, we are conditioned to expect that on a child's chronological birthday he necessarily will be physiologically developed to the same degree as every other child of that particular age.

For example, in Ohio if a child's fifth birthday occurs before October first, he is expected to enter kindergarten. Yet in any given kindergarten classroom, the children may differ in their developmental maturity levels as much as two and one half years. It is common knowledge that the average six-year-old boy is six months behind the average six-year-old girl. The average twelve-year-old boy is developmentally twelve months behind the average twelve-year-old girl. (Some authorities believe that men never do catch up, therefore most men marry younger women!) Despite these differences in maturity, the kindergarten entry date is the same for boys and girls.

Dad, please respect these differences. Not every five-year-old boy or girl is ready for school. Some children need more time to develop. This has nothing to do with intelligence or physical size. Many "late bloomers" are very gifted or large in stature.

Many parents inevitably ask the question, "What can I do to help my youngster catch up?" I generally respond with another question, "What can you do to make your child's second teeth come in sooner?"

Nursery school is not the answer. Preschool experiences are sometimes helpful in providing socialization for children. However, if you have the time or the inclination, you can prepare your child for school just as well, if not

opment. Only the gift of time can accomplish that.

You will not harm a five-year-old youngster by holding him back a year. You can cause him a great deal of anxiety, though, by pushing him into a grade where the curriculum and competition will be overly demanding. Children who are over-placed often become disruptive and disinterested in school in later years. And after first grade, the stigma of retention intensifies. Therefore, the earlier this decision is made in a child's behalf, the better.

If you are interested in pursuing this particular topic further, I suggest the following books: *Don't Push Your Preschooler* by Louise Ames and Dorothy Chase (Harper and Row, 1981) and *School Readiness* by Ilg, Ames, Haines, and Gillespie (Harper and Row, 1978).

GOTTA START SOMETIME

One of the greatest needs we have as human beings is a sense of belonging. For sound mental health, it is absolutely imperative for us to feel that our lives count for something. A child, too, needs to feel that he is an essential, contributing member of the family. In essence, he needs to know that his family couldn't function without him!

One way to convey both belonging and respect is to assign children specific responsibilities. I'll never forget how excited our three-year-old son was when I taught him to change the toilet paper roll. He lit up like a Christmas tree, and we started referring to the task as "Ben's job."

Recently, Ben has trained his younger sister and eager apprentice, Hannah, in the art of "T.P." technology. If we need a new roll and Hannah is not to be found, it's best to find a box of Kleenex. There's a sort of unwritten law mandating that only the bearer of the job has permission to complete the task. Childhood unionization, I believe it's called.

Ben is now the official mirror cleaner, garbage man, and seat buckler. He buckles his sisters in and checks all passengers before we can exit the driveway. I must admit there are times I've attempted to drive unharnessed, but I'm usually found out and sheepishly have to buckle up at the side of the road.

With baby Carolyn now crawling about, the older children also serve as floor inspectors. Any "edible" items they find on the floor are worth a penny—their property excluded. Any item Mom and Dad find is confiscated for a reward.

Of course, you usually want to assign tasks the child can successfully complete. Realistic expectations for both the father and the child are essential.

But there are times, within reason, that a child may wish to tackle a job that seems beyond him. Please remember there is a certain amount of growth in failure. One of the toughest things to do is patiently sit back and keep your mouth shut as your son or daughter fervently struggles with a task you could do for them in a fraction

we wash the car, do the dishes, or paint the woodwork? Our tendency is to very subtly suggest they find something else to do. Then, when they become adolescents and we have a lot of work to be done, we can't find them.

MAKING IT FUN

Most people, including children, need a certain amount of structure to encourage them to assume responsibility. Perhaps you could use a job board with colorful stickers or calendars with a personalized job schedule. Whatever method you employ, be creative and consistent.

During the next week, make a list of things you're doing for your child that he could be doing for himself. If you've just had your firstborn, it's not too early to plan ahead. Depending upon the age of your child, you might encourage him to try the following:

Order for himself at a restaurant
Make his own lunches
Help in planning future meals
Make his own bed
Do the dishes (Any rubber dishes in the house?)
Help select his own clothes to buy and wear
Take the garbage out
Bring the garbage cans back in
Set the table

Wash the floor
Vacuum the floo
Wash the car
Use a tool kit
Empty the waste b
Change the toilet p
Grow his own garde
Mail letters
Use the phone (specifically, learn who to call in an emergency)
Spend and save money

The list is limitless and, as you may have noticed, some of these suggestions include decision-making.

DECISIONS, DECISIONS

Decision-making is a skill that needs to be learned just like any other skill. It is not something you acquire on your eighteenth birthday. Even toddlers can be given opportunities to make decisions. Would you like a hot dog or a peanut butter sandwich? Do you want to wrestle or play ball? Would you like to wear this shirt or that shirt? If our children become comfortable making simple decisions, then they at least have some background for making the more critical ones as they get older.

On school days when Ben buys his lunch, he is given one dollar. Lunch costs eighty cents; ice cream is an additional twenty cents. Ben can decide whether to use the twenty cents for ice cream or to bring it home and save it up for something he really wants. In his case, it's a bicycle speedometer. So far he's been bringing home the change about 50 percent of the time.

GIVING THEM SPACE

Another means of demonstrating respect involves the issue of privacy. Children, as well as their parents, need a healthy amount of privacy. Anytime a bedroom or bathroom door is closed, a knock is required.

Once again, the best way to teach anything is by example. Thus, the most effective way of teaching respect for privacy is to model that behavior. You can be sure that if you're consistent in your efforts, they'll be consistent in theirs. If you knock before entering the bedroom or bathroom, they'll appreciate it and extend you the same courtesy.

This same principle can also apply to telephone conversations and letters in the mail. Eavesdropping or hassling them during their conversation on the phone is as infuriating to children as it would be to you. In written correspondence, a letter written to an individual should be opened by that individual.

In many ways, children today are no different from children of previous generations. They need love, direction, and a sense of belonging. Indeed, the child in each of us needs to feel unique and special.

Generally speaking, however, our society is unconcerned about nurturing anyone else's self-esteem. In fact, the world around us has the unfortunate knack of creating feelings of insecurity. Considering the frequency of negative messages a child receives, it takes a real commitment from parents to counter-balance them.

HAPPY BIRTHDAY

Insecurity and regression often arise following the birth of a sibling. The older child has spent the last few years assuming his identity and establishing his position in the home. Little brother or sister can be perceived as a real threat to that once comfortable position.

Many hospitals are now involving children in the birth process to ease this period of transition. Visiting privileges have been relaxed, sibling preparation classes are taught, and children are treated as responsible contributing members of the family.

When the baby arrives home from the hospital, two key factors are essential in maintaining an effective relationship with your older child. First, Mother and the older child need special time to be alone together in order to continue their unique relationship. Naturally, that infers that Dad and baby will become well-acquainted.

Now I can't honestly say I relish the thought of changing dirty diapers. I will say, however, that the degree to which you are willing to become actively involved not only will benefit your wife and the other children, but also will deepen your relationship with the baby.

Second, the older child has certain wisdom, abilities, and knowledge that can greatly influence the development of the baby's character. Encouraging the older child to see the importance of his position and giving him specific and relevant responsibilities will reduce regression and sibling rivalry. (Sibling rivalry can never be totally eliminated, but these measures can help minimize it.) Some responsibilities for the older child might include the following:

Patting the baby's back for burping purposes
Bringing clean diapers when the baby needs changing
Holding the powder
Helping to make the baby's bed
Unwrapping baby gifts (Include some gifts for the older child!)
Teaching the baby how to hug and kiss
Checking to see if the baby is covered
Singing songs to the baby
Making the baby laugh
Telling or reading stories to the baby
Helping to push the stroller
Introducing the baby to friends and neighbors
Holding the baby when sitting in a special chair

Of course, there are certain rules to be followed as well:

Don't put things in the baby's bed.
Don't put things in the baby's mouth.
Don't climb into the baby's bed.
Be gentle with the baby, particularly his neck, eyes, and soft spot.
Don't try to pick up the baby.
Hold the baby only when you're sitting down in the special chair.

When Mom and baby come home from the hospital, the youngster at home may be excited to see the baby, but Mother is the one he really misses. Handling that reunion in the following way might be helpful.

Have a relative or a close friend take care of the youngster while Dad picks up Mother and baby at the hospital. Settle the new baby in bed, then call for the youngster to be brought home. Mom and Dad can meet the older child at the front door and spend some quality time together without distraction or interference from the infant. When you're ready, go *together* into the baby's room to complete your family reunion.

During the next few weeks and months, most adults will pay particular attention to the baby. Be sure to include your older youngster in the conversation as well. "Jessica has been such a good helper! You should see the way she. . . ." When Carolyn was born, I dubbed three-year-old Hannah as my "Sweet-Sweet." She seemed to like her new nickname, and when she introduced Carolyn, would quickly add, "And I'm Sweet-Sweet." While the other adults ooh and aah over the baby, it's an ideal time to pick up your older youngster for some tender loving care.

HELPING THEM STAND ON THEIR OWN TWO FEET

If we view our parenting role objectively, we have the rather disheartening task of working our way out of a job. In effect, we are carefully shaping these little lives, nurturing them to various levels of independence. They will always appreciate our love and support. However, ultimately each child should have the inner strength, wisdom, and self-confidence to function autonomously by early adulthood.

To fulfill our role, we need to provide appropriate opportunities for growth to occur. At the same time, we need to refrain from reinforcing a child's feelings of inadequacy.

As a four-year-old, Hannah became quite fearful of unfamiliar people and places. She would literally wrap her little body around my leg in a department store or cry hysterically in Sunday school. This was an unpleasant situation for both parent and child. As her father, my emotions ranged from empathy to anger.

This problem was not solved overnight. In fact, it took months for us to alleviate her fears and bolster her self-confidence.

First we enrolled Hannah in a gymnastics class because she had some athletic ability and we wanted to encourage her success in an area of competence. Yet it took weeks for her to work with the instructor without fear and trembling.

At McDonald's, we encouraged Hannah to ask for more ketchup and napkins. Initially, we walked to the counter with her. In time, she became willing to venture out holding her little sister's hand. Finally, she not only accomplished the task on her own but did it with a twinkle in her eye. (We bought a lot of hamburgers in those days!)

We tried a similar approach in mailing letters. After walking her down the street to the mailbox the first few times, we began to wean her by only walking her part of the way. Eventually, she no longer needed our assistance.

Each task was done in a firm, but friendly, manner with such messages as, "I've got confidence in you, honey" and "I know you can do it." Sometimes we referred to this dilemma as a game or a battle. "Hannah, you're playing a game against fear. Who's winning? You can whip that fear, Hannah. You're going to win."

Scripture verses also helped. Hannah memorized Isaiah 12:2, "I will trust and not be afraid," as well as Philippians 4:13, "I can do all things through Him who strengthens me."

It has been a year since Hannah was in the heat of that battle and we are thrilled by her progress. What a delight to watch as she graciously approaches her friends and ours, looks them directly in the eyes, and converses with poise, enjoying every minute.

Parents in the midst of similar situations are invariably burdened with guilt. They feel they are responsible for their child's behavior due to their own inadequacies in child-rearing. This is seldom the case. However, parents play a key role in helping their child conquer the adversary, whatever it may be.

Ben never experienced such an intense bout with insecurity, but we have suffered with him through difficult times of a different sort. His first week of first grade was painful as he adjusted to a full day of school with a more advanced curriculum and a new teacher.

I can still remember tucking him into bed one night as he vowed never to return to school. After listening to him,

I concluded our discussion with this message, "Ben, this is a tough situation, and I think I understand how badly you feel. But if anyone can handle this, *you* are the one. I have confidence in you, buddy. Let me know how it's going for you."

Later that week he forgot his lunch money. Actually, I thought it was courageous of him to even consider buying lunch. You see, most of the young primary students are "packers," especially early in the year. (The fact that the "buyers" line is so threatening still puzzles me.)

Ann called me at my office to share the distressing news. How I wanted to hop into the car, drive to the school, run into the classroom, and place the money in his hands and make everything all better. I reasoned, however, that he was capable of coping with the situation, and my actions should reflect my confidence in his ability. Looking at this situation myopically, I could have solved Ben's problem for him. Yet, in perspective, he then would have missed the satisfaction and growth he experienced by dealing with the matter himself.

Recently we moved into a new house across town. Due to my job in elementary counseling, I knew most of the children in the neighborhood. As I waved to some of the boys down the street, Ben asked me to walk him over and introduce him to the group.

Once again I was torn between accommodating my seven-year-old son and allowing him to tackle a new challenge. After all, introducing yourself to a group of people is a learning experience and sometimes you *learn* best by *doing*.

Therefore, I explained to Ben that this was a chance for him to try something new and, perhaps, difficult. I assured him that he would enjoy the satisfaction of accomplishing this feat and wished him well. After giving the matter some thought, he slowly meandered down the street. Moments later he returned triumphantly, saying, "I did it, Dad. I did it!"

Learning to swim requires entering the pool. Learning to drive requires steering the wheel. Learning to walk requires taking that first big step. Parental discretion is important in determining whether or not a specific venture is appropriate. I do think, however, we often underestimate the capability and resourcefulness of our children.

THE GENERATION GAP: IN ONE ERA AND OUT THE OTHER

Probably the biggest complaint that teenagers voice about their parents relates to a lack of respect. "They don't understand me." "They just don't listen." "They treat me like a baby." "Talking with my Dad is like talking to the wall."

What every youngster wants in a relationship is what every adult wants—acceptance and respect. It is a frightening, but valid, thought that children who don't find acceptance at home will look for it elsewhere. It might be the street corner, a hangout, or someone else's home, but all youngsters seek environments of acceptance.

A recent rock hit proclaimed that we're "just another brick in the wall." What a depressing thought! I sincerely hope our kids don't feel that way in our homes, and I most certainly want to avoid being like a wall. Along the lines of architectural analogies, I much prefer to be seen as an open door.

One way to achieve this openness is to listen first and then let your speech be seasoned with sense and sensitivity. How good it would be to hear an adolescent say, "Dad, you know something? You don't always agree with me, but somehow I think you understand me. Thanks, Dad, I needed that!"

WHAT YOU SAY AND HOW YOU SAY IT

One of the best ways of communicating respect to your children is simply the manner in which you communicate with them. This includes both speaking and listening.

The choice of our words can determine the length and quality of our relationship with another person. Now and then in my counseling with high school students, the problem of teenage pregnancy arises. The young woman who finds herself in this predicament is usually quite nervous and distraught. Her self-image at this point is at an all-time low. What she needs is a good listener to help her sort things through while at the same time preserving her dignity.

Nevertheless, one of my responsibilities is determining who the father is. I could ask, "Do you know who the father is?" But what am I implying? It would be like pouring salt into the wound, and it would more than likely dissolve our relationship.

The same information can be gathered using an approach that is much less offensive. I might say, "Does the father know?" The information is obtained, the relationship is stabilized, and the young mother's self-esteem is not sacrificed.

The same principle can be applied in speaking to our own children. It is all too common when shopping, for instance, to hear abusive adjectives tossed in the face of a wide-eyed youngster. "Stupid," "monster," "brat," "spoiled," "pain in the neck" (or worse) are representative of the labels parents put on children. It's easy to do when you're busy and tired. But we have a rule in our house that no one—parent or child—ever puts down someone else. That's not to say there are not arguments or misunderstandings, but there are *no* put downs.

We can express our concerns to the youngsters without, as James Dobson phrases it in his book, *Hide or Seek*, "crushing the spirit." I can remember as a first grader how I struggled to complete my work. I was the youngest child in the class, and my work very much reflected my immaturity. I tried, but my printing book was a sight. It was smeared and inaccurate, and the letters didn't fit exactly between the lines.

One afternoon, our teacher held up my book in front of the class, severely berated me, and tore up my painstaking work (as well as my heart). As the pieces of paper floated down around me, I fought off the tears and a growing lump in my throat. The dam burst at home later that day.

This happened years ago, but, even as I write, the

memory becomes very clear and alive with emotion. I happened to meet my former teacher some twenty-eight years later. She was old and still seemed very serious and cold. Although I'm certain she didn't remember this episode, I'll never forget it.

Her reaction was unfair, although I was too young to know it. All I knew was that she was right, and I was wrong. She was good, I was bad. She was the teacher, I was the bungling student. But the point is, the problem could have and should have been handled differently. My spirit was crushed at the hands of an insensitive adult. And a crushed spirit leaves scars behind.

My printing was atrocious, I'm sure. It was not deliberate, I just wasn't adept. My teacher's energy would have been better spent in improving my skills or at least recognizing my need to grow at my own speed. My poor penmanship was the issue, but it was my person, my very spirit, that was dealt with.

With this in mind, let's look at a typical home situation and deal with it appropriately. The children are noisily playing and I am trying to listen to the ball game. Now that's a frustrating situation! Normally, their play wouldn't bother me. However, at this point, it is interfering with my needs.

I might react by shouting, "Will you kids shut up!?! How am I supposed to hear the game with all this noise in here?" Or I might just send them to their rooms. Another alternative would be to state, very matter-of-factly, "It's difficult to hear the ball game with all this noise in here."

In the last alternative, I have given my children the opportunity to respect me and my needs.

In Don Dinkmeyer and Gary McKay's book, *The Parent's Handbook* (American Guidance, 1982), they describe this approach as an "I-message." I simply convey how I am affected by the child's behavior, as opposed to sending a "you-message" like "You, shut up!" An I-message does not assure 100 percent cooperation each time it is employed. However, it often works for us and is a good first step. Further steps will be discussed in the chapter on discipline.

I might add that it is also delightfully rewarding to be the recipient of an I-message, especially when your child is the sender. And it will happen! Children watch their dads very closely. They want to be just like them. If we are "screamers," they'll be "screamers." But if we communicate with respect, chances are they will, as well—with you and with others. They have to be taught, and sometimes we do, too.

HONESTY: THE BEST POLICY

A final point in terms of speaking with respect is honesty. It is extremely easy to be casually dishonest with young children. It is often done either inadvertently or to ward off an imminent confrontation. Here are a few examples.

When I'm chewing gum, and my daughter, whom I wish not to have gum at the moment, asks me what I'm eating, I may be inclined to reply, "Broccoli." That certainly would end the discussion! When we're driving by

McDonald's and the kids start having a Big Mac Attack, we may be tempted to say, "It's closed," though the "Open 24 Hours" sign is clearly in sight. When we're shopping and they ask for a Big Bird coloring book, we might claim bankruptcy. We're on the way to the doctor's office for my son's pre-kindergarten physical exam and he asks if a shot is in the works. I might plead ignorance, although I know full well what's in store.

Probably most parents can relate to this white lie syndrome. And yet honesty is something we expect from our children. It seems only right that we be as honest with them as we expect them to be with us. Although it's easier to appease our children for the moment by sacrificing veracity, my wife and I have found it better in the long run to deal squarely with each situation at the moment it arises.

In teaching such abstract qualities as truth and honesty to children, it is necessary to be concrete and simple. When Ben, at age three, told me something I knew to be untrue, we had a conference on the spot. It happened to be in the bathroom. We both sat down on the floor, and I grabbed a bar of soap. I told him to ask me if I had any soap in my hand. It must have seemed an unusual request because I obviously did.

When my reply to the question was "no," his big brown eyes widened with concern. I explained the fact that what I had just told him was a lie. I assured him I would never lie to him again. We repeated the process and this time, to his relief, I told the truth—something he could count on from me and something I expected from him.

HE WHO HAS AN EAR, LET HIM HEAR

The other end of communication is listening. The Simon and Garfunkel hit of the sixties, "The Sounds of Silence," speaks of people hearing without listening. Do you know anyone like this? As you attempt to speak with him, he turns you right off, verbally and nonverbally.

Parents often complain, "Johnny never tells me anything. I've tried everything to find out what's going on in school, but all I get out of him is an occasional grunt." This is a very common problem, especially for parents of teenagers. This difficult period of transition may have something to do with the introspection characteristic of many adolescents. However, check out some communication "stoppers" and look closely at two possibilities.

First, what can I do to open up lines of communication and foster a better relationship with my youngster? Second, what am I inadvertently doing that my kids might see as a roadblock to communication?

When someone is speaking, it is vitally important to feel that the listener is *really* listening. Some authorities call it "active" listening. Others term it "reflective" listening. It is simply assuring the speaker that we care about what he is saying.

In active listening, we not only hear what the speaker is saying, but we look for feelings behind the content of his words. Finally, we empathize with him, trying to feel and understand what he is sharing. Just as a mirror reflects a physical image, reflective listeners mirror an emotional image to the speaker. The speaker, in effect, has his words and feelings clarified for him by the listener.

Active listening is an art and a very precious one. How many good listeners do you know? How many people actually take time to hear what you're saying? Those who do make you feel good. They become genuinely involved in hearing you out. What you're saying is important to them. They are special people because they make you feel special. I can't think of a better way to demonstrate respect for another person than by actively listening *with* him.

We can demonstrate our desire to listen actively through good eye contact. With children, that means sitting down at eye level. Can you imagine what it's like talking with somebody three feet taller than you? Facial expressions and body language are also good stimulators of conversation. By nodding your head occasionally, smiling, leaning forward, or giving a loving touch, you will assure your child of your genuine interest.

Of course, effective listening is best accomplished when we have ample time and can give our undivided attention. It's a little disconcerting to converse with someone who's forever looking at his watch.

Nevertheless, there will be many times when your child needs to talk and you honestly haven't the time at that moment. You might respond, "It sounds like you really need to talk this out, and I'm interested in working it through with you. I have a meeting in half an hour. How would it be if we meet together after supper tonight at 6:30?"

You may find that by 6:30 there is no longer a problem. But at least the opportunity was given.

A TIME TO SPEAK AND A TIME TO BE SILENT

I think it would be fair to say that most parents talk too much. There are times when a child needs you just to listen and reflect. Sometimes we are too eager to advise when what our child really needs is someone to merely help him understand his own feelings. Conversely, as fathers, we are in a position where our advice, guidance, and direction are necessary factors in our children's development. Knowing which to provide is a matter of discernment. As Kenny Rogers sings,

> You gotta know when to hold 'em,
> Know when to fold 'em,
> Know when to walk away,
> Know when to run.

Sensitivity is the key. There are times when advice should be provided. There are other situations in which simple reflective listening is the better approach.

Remember, in reflective listening you're concerned with both content and feeling. Reword what your child stated with a feeling word, if appropriate, and send it back to him. This will enable him to better understand himself.

The following is an example of a conversation combining reflective listening and guidance.

> *Son:* I really don't want to go to soccer practice anymore.
> *Dad:* Sounds like you're discouraged about soccer.
> *Son:* Yeah. It's just not any fun lately.
> *Dad:* You don't like it as much as you used to?

Son: No! Now Coach Phillips has me playing goalie, and I mostly stand around and I really don't know what I'm doing.

Dad: You weren't happy about being moved to goalie because it's scary playing a new position.

Son: Dad, I feel like a jerk out there. I love soccer, but goalie is not for me.

Dad: Sounds like you'd like to stay with it, but just change positions.

Son: Right.

Dad: Well, what are your alternatives at this point?

Dad could have jumped on his son's first statement of wanting to quit soccer. He might have lectured him about never quitting, or he might have been critical in a number of other ways. But without really listening, he never would have understood his son's dilemma.

Of course, had the conversation continued, Dad would have assisted his son in considering various alternatives and selecting the most appropriate one. Nevertheless, it took active listening and nonjudgmental responses on Dad's part to even reach the point of considering alternatives.

LOOK FOR CUES

As you actively listen to your children, it is often helpful to look for nonverbal clues about their disposition at the moment. Sometimes what they say and what you see are two entirely different messages.

One sunny day Ben and I were both on the playground

at school. I noticed a great number of children were looking through the fence into a neighboring backyard. When Ben saw me, he jumped out of his swing and excitedly ran to me. We talked for a moment, then I asked him what was going on over by the fence. He immediately shifted his feet, turned his head, and said, "I don't know."

"You don't know or you'd rather not tell me?" I questioned softly.

"I'd rather not tell you," he sighed.

"That's OK," I responded. "You can tell me some other time if you want to."

Moments later he came over and divulged the great attraction at the fence. As I bent over, he whispered in my ear, "Some lady is half-naked in her bathing suit over there!"

It was once written that the eyes are the window of the soul. By focusing on the eyes of the other person, we can determine a great deal about the way he is processing the conversation. For example, when a person rolls his eyes up or looks skyward, he is processing thoughts and ideas. When the eyes focus in a downward position or the head is bowed, the person is generally searching for feelings. Closed eyes might simply indicate that the conversation at this point has touched on a topic that is very difficult to discuss. The shifting of feet or looking away might also signify that you, indeed, have struck a nerve.

In our playground situation, Ben initially stated he didn't know what the kids were looking at, but his body language spoke loudly to the contrary. Although I had picked up on the double message, it was essential that I be sensitive in my confrontation rather than mercilessly bludgeoning him with the truth.

There are no real earth-shattering revelations here. As a matter of fact, much of this advice is so-called common sense. Unfortunately, although common sense may be very sensible, it is far too uncommon.

TAKING STOCK: RESPECT

Some dads feel good about themselves but have difficulty communicating respect for others in the family. Other dads highly respect their wife and children, but their own self-esteem is in jeopardy. Perhaps you are a father who possesses a healthy self-image and conveys equal respect to other family members. Try to determine which of the following descriptions best fits you, then write your response in the space provided.

1 ____________
I feel good about myself as a father, and I consistently display an equally high degree of respect for the other family members.

2 ____________
I'm somewhere between #1 and #3.

3 ____________
I highly respect the other family members. However, I have very little confidence as a father. My self-esteem is hurting.

4 ____________
I'm somewhere between #3 and #5.

5 ____________
I have poor self-esteem, and I'm afraid I don't have much respect for the other family members either.

6 ____________
I'm somewhere between #5 and #7.

7 ____________
I respect myself as a father, but I don't regard the other family members with the same degree of respect.

8 ____________
I'm somewhere between #7 and #1.

Dad's response: ______________________________

____

Now ask your wife or another family member to guess which number you selected. In addition, ask them to determine which one they feel best describes you. Then discuss your conclusions in a positive and constructive way.

Wife's guess of Dad's response: ________________

____

Wife's view of Dad's position: _________________

____

If your response was #1, you are functioning in the ideal position. If your response was something other than #1, perhaps some of the material in this chapter will enable you to feel better about yourself and others. Regardless of how you scored, use the space below to set a goal to maintain or improve your present position. It would be wise to list some specific action steps as well.

Dad's goal: __________________________________

____

Action steps: ________________________________

____

____

____

____

It is usually most profitable if you select an "advocate," such as a family member or close friend, to encourage you with your goal on a regular basis and to assist you in evaluating your progress.

THREE

Love: No "Ifs," "Ands," or "Buts"

IF ever a term was abused, misused, and confused, surely "love" would take the prize. Our society uses the word so freely that the potency it once possessed has been diluted.

The elusive nature of the term was probably best captured by the ancient Greeks. They utilized three different words to describe the different types of love.

Eros was the word used for love in conjunction with sexual attraction. The derivation of the word, erotic, lingers on in the marquees of various burlesque and pornographic establishments across the country.

Phileo, as in "Philadelphia," denoted friendship and brotherly love. It also was used to express a love for things. For example, I love to go camping, or I love apple pie.

Agape love had the deepest meaning of the three. *Eros* pertained to the body, *phileo* dealt with the soul, but *agape* related to the spirit of the inner person.

Agape is the type of love that seeks someone else's good at your own expense. It is a godly, unconditional love. Whereas society's version of love insists, "I will love you if. . . ," "I will love you but. . . ," or "I will love you when. . . ," agape love assures, "I love you, period." It's an unconditional love, ever present, regardless of performance or behavior.

As Fathers, our love and regard for our children needs to be absolute, never changing, only intensifying as they grow older. Nothing anyone can do, no circumstance that may arise, should cause this love to be diminished.

UNCONDITIONAL LOVE

About an hour's drive from our home is a beautiful amusement park, Cedar Point. Each summer we go as a family and thoroughly enjoy ourselves. One July morning as we approached the huge parking area and saw the magnificent Ferris wheel silhouetted against the summer sky, Hannah's excitement could no longer be contained. She flew across the front seat, threw her little arms around my neck, and screamed, "You're a good Daddy. I love you."

Well, quite honestly, this was a bittersweet experience. It was sweet in the sense that my little girl had expressed her love to me. It was bitter because her affection coincided with our arrival at Cedar Point. It means so much more to receive this expression of love when I'm not doing anything special. In the same way, a child needs to feel he is special apart from achievement and performance.

There is tremendous security in knowing you are loved just because you are who you are. Our task as fathers is to get this message across to our children with unmistakable clarity.

We are so conditioned to feel that our merit as individuals depends upon performance. Certainly performance is important, but a child's self-esteem should never be sacrificed at the altar of performance. Grades depend upon performance. Money often depends upon performance. Winning or losing depends upon performance.

But your love for your children (and your wife, for that matter) should never be based upon performance. And although we may not intend it as such, sometimes our children perceive it in this way. When children grow up feeling that our love and regard for them is less than absolute, it generates feelings of insecurity. That is why the moments we share our love or show our pride should not be reserved for specific demonstrations of good behavior.

If my daughter brings home straight 'A's' on her report card and I flower her at that moment with "I'm so proud of you" and "I love you," what might she infer? "In order to get my Daddy's love and affection, I need to get good grades."

Certainly, we would be happy for her and appreciative of her hard work. And we should tell her so. However, the most meaningful time to express affection is when it's least expected. What we want our children to internalize is that their Daddy loves them just because they are his children. Indeed, just because they *are*.

That's not to say we accept their misbehavior. Certainly misbehavior needs to be corrected. But our positive regard for our child should not vary according to our disposition at the moment of his misbehavior. In effect, unconditional love says there's nothing you can do to make me love you more. There's nothing you can do to make me love you less.

We play a little game at home to reinforce the consistent nature of our love in the minds of our children. At unexpected moments, perhaps as we're wrestling around, I say, "Who loves you anyhow?" My children have learned to respond immediately, "Daddy." If a stranger on the street were to ask them the same question, even then they would respond, "Daddy!"

I know of a man who, in a similar way, asks his children, "What are you good for anyway?" The conditioned response is "Loving." There will be rough days ahead when these kids face rejection, disappointment, and despair. Hopefully, as they think to themselves, "Who loves me?" and "What am I good for?" the words "Daddy" and "Loving" will come to mind.

FAMILY TIME

Family time is necessary to keep the lines of communication open and strengthen family ties. It can revolve around any activity, from camping to shopping. It also can be regularly scheduled on a daily or weekly basis. It may be as structured as a family meeting, or as informal as a drive in the country It may range in purpose from problem solving to prayer and Bible study. The length and focus of your time together will depend largely on the age of your children.

The following is a brief list of open-ended topics you might use in a family discussion:

1. What one change would you like to make in your life?
2. Name your best friend and tell what you like about him.
3. What is your most prized possession?
4. Who is the person or character you would most like to have dinner with?
5. What is your earliest memory?
6. (At any holiday) What is your best or most vivid memory of this holiday from a previous year?
7. (At any holiday) What does this holiday mean to you?
8. (Anytime, but definitely at Thanksgiving) "I'm thankful for. . . ." (You might go several times around the family circle, letting each person complete the thought in a variety of ways).
9. (On vacation) What is your most vivid memory of a past vacation?
10. What was the worst thing that happened at school or work this week?
11. What was the best thing that happened at school or at work this week?
12. What is one thing you'd like to learn to do better?

13. What is one thing you'd like to learn to do?
14. What is one thing you'd do differently if you did today over?

ONE-ON-ONE TIME

In addition to family time, children need to have time alone with each parent. Probably the best time for this is bedtime. If possible, stagger the bedtimes of your children and spend the last twenty minutes of the day with them one-on-one. You may want to read with them, play a quiet game, or just talk. (The TV, radio, and stereo should be turned off.) Bedtime is often a mellow time in which to reflect on the accomplishments or frustrations of the day.

Spending time alone with your child keeps your relationship alive and well. There's no substitute for just talking at bedtime or running an errand together.

Actually, these informal times of rubbing shoulders with our children are much more conducive to quality communication than when we make them sit under the bright kitchen lights and tell us everything that happened in school that day. Simply driving in the car together is much more likely to invite conversation than a planned meeting in a formal setting.

A beautiful park system is located near our home. Each of the children and I have designated a special spot where the two of us can go to spend time together. Ben's spot is next to a little waterfall, Hannah's is on a hill under some pine trees, and Carolyn's is beside a covered bridge. It's a special spot for a special tot—and Dad.

Praying aloud with your child is a terrific means of

building self-esteem as well as spiritual understanding. For example, my prayer with Carolyn might include the following statements. "Heavenly Father, I thank you for Carolyn. I thank you for her joyful spirit and her tender heart. I appreciate that you chose me to be her Daddy to love and guide her. Give me wisdom and patience, and help me express to her each day just how much you and I both love her."

TIME IS OF THE ESSENCE

Unfortunately, family and individual times rarely just happen. Most of us live life in the fast lane, and important matters must be scheduled. Take time to make time with your family. Keep it a priority.

An aggravating idea about time is commonly published in various psychology and parenting publications. They advocate, almost universally, that not the quantity but the quality of time you spend with your children is important. Certainly, both quantity and quality are important. However, in my estimation, quality time has been rationalized to a point where it almost borders on neglect.

Imagine ordering a filet mignon at a high-class restaurant with high-class prices. When the waiter returns, he sets before you a cut of meat about the size of a large olive. When you complain (and quite rightfully so) about the amount of steak prepared for you, the waiter matter-of-factly declares it's not the quantity but the quality that really counts. That's about as ridiculous as telling my son I only have ten minutes for him this week, but we'll make it quality time. Big deal!

A difficult aspect of scheduling time for our families is its apparent conflict with our careers. About the time your children need you most is usually the time you are becoming very productive at work. These are crucial years of advancement and promotion.

I would encourage you to take a good, hard look at your priorities. The job is important, but if we're not careful, it can become a runaway racehorse. All of the money in the world can't turn back the clock, and your kids are kids only for a short time.

A DOSE OF HUMILITY

One of the most difficult tasks for any of us is admitting when we're wrong. For some reason, we stumble over the words, and sometimes they never do come out. Either that, or we rationalize our behavior to the point where we're convinced we were justified for whatever we did or said. The problem is that whoever was wronged or wrongfully accused never forgets. Bitterness and resentment bury themselves at the subconscious level.

I remember hearing the story of a youngster who was severely reprimanded for leaving his father's tools out in the rain. Later that evening, the father walked past the tree under which the tools had been forgotten. In a crevice of the trunk, he spotted the pipe tobacco he had stashed while working with the misplaced tools. Instantly, the father recalled that he was actually the guilty party.

His son was anxiously watching from the window. When his father returned to the house, the boy hoped for an apology. But there was never a word. The incident was over, but not forgotten—at least not by the boy.

Admitting we're wrong merely administers a healthy dose of humility to us. It does not threaten our authority. On the contrary, it actually magnifies our children's respect for us.

One afternoon a principal apologized to the student body over the public address system for a mistaken assumption on his part. Rather than generating a disgruntled "I told you so" attitude on the part of the students, the incident noticeably increased their fondness for this man.

TO FORGIVE IS DIVINE

The same principle applies to forgiveness. Too often we bring up the past to our children. Issues should be dealt with squarely, then forgiven and forgotten.

At breakfast one morning, Ben, who was three at the time, inadvertently spilled my glass of juice. That particular morning, I must have crawled out on the right side of the bed. In response to his "I'm sorry, Daddy," I graciously replied, "That's OK, buddy. It was an accident."

Not two hours later, I stumbled over his tower of wooden building blocks. Before I could think to say I'm sorry, he smiled up at me and said, "That's OK, Daddy. It was an accident." I always wonder how he would have handled the demolition of his castle if I had reacted differently at breakfast.

LOVING THEIR MOTHER

One of the most effective means of demonstrating love for children is by loving their mother. A foundation of warmth and security is built in a home where the love relationship between a husband and wife is healthy. Both parents are uniquely special to children, and each child identifies with both Mother and Dad. That's why put-down statements between parents directly affect the youngster. If Mom is being ridiculed or belittled, a child takes it personally.

This is an especially sensitive issue in situations where Mom and Dad have separated or divorced. Often the tendency is to involve children in the great debate of innocence and guilt, virtue and immorality. When Mom has the kids, she drags Father through the mud, subtly or otherwise. Of course, Dad returns the favor when the opportunity presents itself.

The child sees himself as part Mom and part Dad. If Dad is "lazy and shiftless" and Mother is a "tramp," imagine the effect on the child's self-image. Parents, even in a difficult divorce situation, it is advisable to forgive and forget. Harboring resentment and malice has little effect on the other parent, but can be devastating to the children.

Love is a wonderfully vital quality in any relationship. It should be absolute, consistent, and openly shared. For generations, the macho male assumed that his wife and children knew he loved them. Gentle talk and physical displays of affection were relegated to the suspect and weak. But men, women, and especially children need to be told as well as shown that they are loved.

The latest research indicates that the biggest variable in a child's healthy sexual development is the presence of a loving and nurturant father. In homes where Dad is openly affectionate with his children, girls tend to be more secure in their femininity and boys more secure in their masculinity. The greatest maternal influence on a child's sexual identity is the mother's attitude towards men in general. If Mother regards men in a favorable light, it will have a positive effect on each child's sexuality.

LOVE MAKES THE DIFFERENCE

Love is said to make the world go around. The world of the baby and toddler consists almost entirely of immediate family. In this fresh, new world, children thrive on love. Studies have verified this fact.

In Great Britain during World War II, orphaned children were cared for by doctors, nurses, and volunteers. Although they were regularly fed, changed, bathed, and given adequate time for sleep, the mortality rate was unusually high. Authorities soon came to realize that these little ones needed to be held, caressed, talked to, and loved. Subsequently, more time was given for these purposes, and the mortality rate was reduced.

As children grow, the way in which we express our love may vary, but the need is ever-present. Adolescents, striving for independence and adulthood, may appear aloof and indifferent. Nevertheless, behind that self-made facade lies the heart of a child yearning to be held and loved. Don't we all!

One of the qualities I most appreciate in my wife, Ann,

is her special attentiveness and kindness early in the morning. This is especially impressive because I know by nature she is not a "morning" person. Each day as the children arise one by one and shuffle into the kitchen, she welcomes them as though they've been away on an extended vacation. You can see the sleepy, yet excited look of anticipation as they peek around the corner until she notices them. What a great way to start off the day. Special K, Corn Flakes, or even Cap'n Crunch can't match it!

Breakfast fulfills our physical needs, but warm and loving words nurture the spirit. And what better time or place to nurture the spirit of a child than early in the morning in your own home?

There is no substitute for genuine, honest-to-goodness love. It is a prerequisite for mental health, the very foundation of an abundant life. Love overcompensates for error-prone parents who fail in their daily attempts to be wise and effective. You can learn about techniques and teach doctrines of truth, but love is a gift. It is a fruit of the Spirit that grows in proportion to that which we give.

TAKING STOCK: LOVE

Many dads have a difficult time expressing love to their children. Some dads avoid talking about love, but they treat their children lovingly and expect that the message is clear. For others, expressing love aloud occurs naturally and frequently. Select which of the following numbers best describes you.

1

I love my children, but I have a difficult time expressing my feelings. It's something I don't do well, and I really haven't worked at it yet.

2

I'm somewhere between #1 and #3.

3

I love my children and I think I'm expressing it appropriately, but I'm not sure. I'm probably showing love by the way I treat them, but I don't come out and say it enough.

4

I'm somewhere between #3 and #5.

5

I love my children and enjoy expressing my love verbally and nonverbally. I am confident in my love relationship with my kids.

Dad's response: ______________________________

____

____

____

It might be interesting to ask your wife to guess which number you selected. Then ask her to determine which number she feels best describes you. Some interesting and profitable discussion can result if this is approached in a positive and constructive way.

Wife's guess of Dad's response: ______________________

____

____

Wife's view of Dad's position: ______________________

____

Obviously #5 would be the ideal response. If your response was not #5, you are to be commended for your honesty. Now what specifically can you do to move in the direction of #5? Perhaps as you read through this chapter you found some specific ideas to help you achieve a more open and loving relationship. Regardless of how you scored, use the space below to set your goal. Your goal could be to maintain your love relationship with your child or to improve it. Then list the specific steps you plan to use to accomplish your goal.

Dad's goal: ______________________________

____

Action steps: ____________________________

____

____

____

____

Sometimes it is helpful to select an advocate, such as your wife or a close friend, to encourage you toward your goal. It is also a good idea to evaluate your progress from time to time.

FOUR

Discipline: It's Not a Dirty Word

THE discipline of children has become a controversial issue in recent years. Permissive approaches to parenting became increasingly prevalent beginning in the fifties and sixties. We were subjected to the notion that parental direction and limit-setting were detrimental to a child's creativity. Dr. Spock, although often misquoted and misunderstood, was a forerunner of permissive parenting.

We are still bombarded with the concept of children's rights and equality. Recent newspaper articles have referred to children suing their parents and laws advocating such atrocities as the legalization of sexual relations involving children. Authority figures in every facet of life are under seige.

Nevertheless, I believe without question that at the very core of our human nature lies a basic need for a sense of order. As I mentioned in chapter 2, equality in terms of worth is not tantamount to equality in terms of role, function, or position. Without some system of structure bearing this premise, individual insecurity and societal chaos will surely emerge. Any tribe or culture on earth that continues to thrive today evidences the presence of a structure of authority.

The bottom line for fathers is this: children desperately need to be assured that you care enough to mean what you say and will back it up with action. They can readily sense a lack of consistency and confidence in your approach to discipline. Although they progressively strive for independence (and should be encouraged to do so), children want the security of knowing that the limits you have set are firm, fair, consistent, and clear.

When I was a coach, I occasionally experienced the aggravation of dealing with an inferior official. Ninety-nine percent of these diligent gentlemen with thankless jobs do a tremendous job of controlling the tempo of the game and the integrity of play. But in some games, coaches and players alike grew frustrated when everything was called very closely in one quarter, and anything went in the next. "Hey, ref, what's it gonna be?"

Well, Dad, what's it gonna be? What are the rules, and what is your game plan for enforcing them? What are your expectations for your child? Are they clear in his mind and in your own? Are the rules thought through, or simply those you had as a child? Do you have a system by which you can *act* responsibly in a given situation, or do you just *react* emotionally according to your disposition at the moment? These are questions that warrant some answers.

CHANGING OUR PERSPECTIVE

A nearby institution deals with the parents of children who are deemed incorrigible and behaviorally or emotionally disturbed. One of the techniques it employs is to videotape the interactions of a parent and child. For instance, a father and his child are placed in a room with various toys and games. Father is instructed to engage the child in a certain activity, then convince the child to switch to a different activity on cue.

More often than not, this is what happens. Dad gets out the building blocks and Junior begins building. The child's behavior is appropriate, and Father picks up a magazine and begins to read. When Junior deviates from his required task or will not switch activities on cue, Dad puts aside his reading materials and coaxes him back to the blocks. They play together awhile, then, when he gets his child back to the task, Dad goes back to his seat, picks up the copy of *Sports Illustrated,* and begins to read.

Notice the process and the implications for Junior. In order to get my father's attention, he reasons, I must misbehave. The attention of an angry father is better than no attention at all.

Encouraging a child when he is behaving appropriately is every bit as important as correcting him when he isn't. In educational circles this technique is often referred to as "cueing." It works something like this.

The teacher walks into a relatively noisy classroom of second graders. Rather than focusing in on the misbehaving children, she instead speaks to a child who is modeling desirable behavior. She might say, "Oh, I like the way Liane is working!" or "I really appreciate how quietly Paul is doing his work. Thank you, Paul!" The child who is doing well gets the teacher's attention, as he should.

In your home, look for positive behavior and respond to it. You'll be surprised at how quickly every child will want that same positive attention.

It's amazing that something so simple would work that effectively. But it does! Staff members of the previously mentioned school for disruptive children indicated that the two most effective techniques in modifying a child's behavior were ignoring the misbehavior and "cueing" desirable behavior. In short, it is far more effective to encourage children when they are behaving appropriately than to discipline them when they aren't.

STEP-BY-STEP

The whole spectrum of discipline is essentially a teaching process. We are teaching such things as right from wrong, respect for self and others, self-control, and good listening skills, to name a few. It is a matter of building character.

Too often, however, the spirit of a child is sacrificed in the name of discipline. Our focus should be directed to the misbehavior, not to the character, as we preserve the dignity of the child and resume our continued love for him.

Earlier we discussed the I-message with reference to

respectfully approaching a child. Let's look at ways to incorporate it effectively in a disciplinary context.

The problem: Your son has left his new ball glove out in the rain.

First step (I-message): "It really disappoints me to see your new ball glove left out in the rain because it cost quite a bit of money."

First recurrence: "I see the ball glove was left out again. I guess you aren't responsible enough to use it properly. You may have it again in three days, and we'll see how you do then."

If the ball glove is returned and eventually left out again, extend the period of time the mitt is to be off-limits.

Notice that the initial length of time the child may not use the glove is relatively short. Most parents make the mistake of grounding or denying privileges for an unrealistic period of time. "OK, buddy, that's it! You go to your room and don't come out until grade cards come out again in six weeks!"

The problem: You are reading and the kids are creating disturbances in your general vicinity.

First step (I-message): "It's really tough to read this book with all this noise in here."

First recurrence: "You've got a choice, Lynn. You may stay in here and play quietly, or go outside and play. You decide."

Second recurrence: "I guess you've decided to go outside and play." (Take her there if necessary.)

Notice the focus of discipline is the child's behavior, not the child herself.

When we are walking in a parking lot, the first thing two-year-old Carolyn wants to do is run. I need to structure the situation by providing her with a choice of two alternatives, either of which would be acceptable to me.

For example, I might say, "Carolyn, do you want to hold my hand, or do you want me to carry you?" I know she usually does not want to be carried, and generally she responds, "Hol' your han'." This is effective a great deal of the time. If she were to run again, however, I would matter-of-factly pick her up and carry her, assuming that she has chosen the other alternative.

Even before Carolyn turned two, this technique was effective. One cold, snowy winter day we were playing in the backyard, and she removed the hood of her snowsuit. I told her I was afraid she would get cold and sick if she took her hood off, and I carefully tied it up for her. Moments later I noticed she had taken the hood off again. This time I asked her if she wanted to play inside with her hood off or outside with her hood on. "Ou'side!" she declared without hesitation.

Yet the inevitable occurred. The hood came down, and Daddy carried her into the house. I went back outside for a few minutes, leaving a sobbing snow baby by the door. I reentered minutes later and asked if she was ready to play outside with her hood up. She understood perfectly and nodded her consent. We enjoyed a solid hour of snow play with happy hearts and warm heads.

CONFLICT RESOLUTION

As I mentioned earlier, responsibilities are important to a child's development. They provide many necessary learning experiences. Unfortunately, they can also be a real source of conflict and irritation.

Mom and Dad decide it's time for seven-year-old Andrew to assume the responsibility of feeding the dog. The only problem is that Mom and Dad find themselves continually reminding, coaxing, and nagging Andrew. Sometimes the dilemma provokes Mom to scream, "Andrew, if you don't feed that dog, he's going to die!" Meanwhile, Dad is thinking, "I'm so sick of this, if you don't feed the dog ***you're*** going to die!"

Mom and Dad rant and rave—and eventually feed the dog themselves. After all, it's easier to give in than to fight.

Why do we so often continue in this way when it obviously doesn't work? Let's stop for a moment and consider a way to handle this situation that would accomplish two objectives. First, we want Andrew to ***fully*** assume his responsibility. In addition, we want to keep a measure of peace in the home.

Dad: "Andrew, whose job is it to feed the dog?"

Andrew: "Mine."

Dad: "Yes, but when I remind you over and over, whose job am I making it?"

Andrew: "Yours, I guess."

Dad: "Yes, Andy, and I'll bet sometimes you wish I'd get off your back."

Andrew: "For sure!"

Dad: "Well, I want you to know that I won't bug you about this anymore."

Andrew: "You won't?"

Dad: "No, Andy, it's all yours. All I want you to know is that Molly needs to be fed between the time you get home from school, 4:00 P.M., and dinnertime, 6:00 P.M."

Andrew: "Are we finished, Dad?"

Dad: "Just one more thing, Andy. Normally each table setting is complete with plates and silverware. However, if Molly hasn't been fed by 6:00 P.M., there will be no plate set for you because you don't eat until the dog eats."

The important thing at this point is consistency and follow-through.

Another source of conflict might be room-cleaning time. This common problem in families so often results in absolute frustration. It's been said that no child has ever died of a dirty room, but some parents have! Let's see how Dad might survive by effectively handling this dilemma.

Dad: "Elizabeth, tomorrow morning is Saturday. Do you know what that means?"

Elizabeth: "Yeah, no school!"

Dad: "Well, that's right. But it also means Saturday morning cleanup."

Elizabeth: "Oh, Dad!"

Dad: "Now what would we consider a clean room?"
Elizabeth: "I don't know . . . bed made, I guess."
Dad: "Good. Go on."
Elizabeth: "Dirty clothes in the hamper, stuff back on the shelves, no dirt on the floor."
Dad: "Great thinking, Beth. Now I want you to know cleanup is a morning project. In other words, morning is over when the room is completed.

"Some kids like their mornings to be relatively short, and others like their mornings to last all day long. I don't really care how long your morning lasts, Beth. I just want you to know that TV, telephone, and lunch are post-morning experiences. Enjoy your week-end, honey." (Dad gives her a wink and a warm smile.)

Please note that the manner in which you present these alternatives to children is very important. If you come on strong and appear to relish getting the upper hand, it will be taken as punishment. If you work conflict through with love and logic, it is accepted more readily.

The following excerpt presents another means of conflict resolution. It is taken from Paul Meier's *Christian Child Rearing and Personality Development* (Baker, 1977).

> Have a two-hour family session involving only the teenager and both parents. Reevaluate all the rules, chores, and punishments objectively. Have the teenager draw a line down the middle of a blank sheet of

paper. Tell him to put specific rules and chores he thinks he should have on the left side of the line, and the punishments he thinks he should receive for breaking each of the rules on the right side. (Surprisingly, most teenagers will be harder on themselves than their parents would have been. Wanting more controls, teenagers frequently break rules so the parents will make them a little stricter.) Then go over each of the rules, chores, and punishments he has listed and discuss them. If they are reasonable, leave them as they are. If they are too strict or too lenient, change the ones you must. As usual, the father should have the ultimate say. When you have completed the list, both parents should sign it and the teenager should also sign it and date it. This becomes a contract between the teenager and his parents. When he lists the chores, tell him to be specific about the day of the week on which he plans to do each chore. If he lives up to his part of the contract, there will be absolutely no need to nag him. If he doesn't keep his part of the bargain, you still won't need to nag—just automatically give him the consequence he listed on the right side of the line. If he breaks a rule, he suffers the consequence he agreed upon. Make the contract good for about a two-month period, and have weekly family meetings to discuss how things are going. Show respect for the teenager as a young adult, and listen to what he has to say, even if you disagree with him. When the two months are up, renegotiate the contract. If he has done a good job, give him a little more freedom in the new contract. If he has done a poor job, make the new contract a little stricter. But do your best to keep the communications constructive and positive, and be sure to compliment your teenager for showing responsibility. I have used this technique scores of times with teenagers and their parents, and the families have usually felt that it helped eliminate much of the negative communications between the parents and the teenager. It also helps put the brakes on the traditional parent-teenager power struggle, and at the same time acknowledges the teenager as a person by valuing his opinions on the rules he ought to have.

WHO'S RUNNING THE SHOW?

When children verbally attack a parent or willfully refuse to comply with a parent's directive, the I-message is probably inappropriate. For example, you've told your three-year-old to pick up her toys. She responds, "No. I don't have to," or "You pick them up," or looks at you and walks away. She's checking your limits and challenging your authority.

In these situations, and these only, spanking is recommended. Your daughter needs to understand that you really are in charge. You can matter-of-factly (not in anger) take her aside, tell her you love her too much to allow her to exhibit this behavior, then proceed with one of the most difficult tasks we will be called upon to administer. It really does hurt us more than it does them! I never understood that as a child, but I've been enlightened in recent years.

The spanking should never be dealt anywhere other than the bottom or the backs of the legs. One or two whacks is sufficient, squarely dealt but not abusive. Many psychologists recommend using a neutral object (i.e., a wooden spoon, paddle, or fly swatter), the basic reason being that children should fear the object but not your hand. Personally, I don't always carry a wooden spoon, paddle, or fly swatter around with me. Furthermore, if the relationship between a parent and child is a good one, there is no apprehension about the intentions of Daddy's hands. There are no surprises. The children know what to expect and when.

You will find that after a spanking is one of the best times for reaffirming your child's worth. He should not escape to the other parent for pity and condolences. This is a very private matter between one parent and one child. A spanking should be carried out in privacy, not witnessed by friends, neighbors, strangers, or family. Think of it in terms of how you'd like to be treated by your boss at work. If your boss felt you needed to be reprimanded, you would not expect him to do it in the presence of your fellow workers.

Spanking in any other way, or for reasons other than defiance, is probably inappropriate and ineffective. It often is the reaction of a frustrated parent with nerves on edge and patience on empty. Before you do anything ask yourself, "Is he deliberately defying me?" Perhaps he didn't hear you, he forgot what you told him, or he had an accident. When you pause to evaluate the misbehavior, the motive, and your response, it's as good as counting to ten.

Of course, if children are disciplined appropriately in their formative years, they seldom need to be, nor should they be, spanked as they grow older. Probably the ages of two to five are the most effective for this kind of discipline. From this point on, the three-step method seems to be most effective. Initially, send an "I message." Next, create a choice. Finally, follow through with the consequence.

The father who seems to have the most difficulty in effectively disciplining his children is the dad who as a child had a very poor love relationship with his parents. This child grows up to be an adult who subconsciously equates discipline with hate and anger. He mistakenly believes that disciplining his children will cause them to dislike him in the same way he dislikes his parents. It is important for Father to understand that discipline, handled appropriately, is an act of love.

AVOIDING THE GUILT TRIP

Along with the accelerated interest and emphasis on parenting, and possibly even as a consequence of it, many conscientious parents are carrying around a load of emotional baggage known as guilt. Each of us has lost his temper with a youngster, unmercifully blasting him with a barrage of words and thunder. Then at night, while he innocently slumbers, we wonder how in the world it could have happened. He's sleeping like an angel, and we feel like the devil.

I remember one night I felt so guilty about unfairly berating little Hannah that I awakened her to apologize. Half asleep, she responded with these words of consolation, "That's OK, Daddy, you're jus' a Daddy and all Daddies prob'ly do that."

When our actions produce long-term consequences, our guilt may be much more intense and difficult to handle. Broken marriages and wayward children can create tremendous and unmanageable burdens.

Recently I heard an interesting analogy that spoke to my heart about this critical issue. It pertains to the Father and children who once resided in the Garden of Eden. Consider the implications of what transpired within this family.

Yet isn't God a perfect Father? Yes, I believe he is *the* perfect Father. Then did the children of the perfect Father turn out perfectly? Absolutely not! Did they make foolish and selfish decisions? Yes, and they even made some miserable excuses in a feeble attempt to justify their actions. The perfect Father had imperfect children!

God could have designed robotic children with no autonomous minds or wills. He could have programmed them to bow at his feet three times daily. He could have removed the Tree of Life and its temptations. But he created children capable of loving or hating, obeying or defying. Throughout their lives, our children will make choices and judgments. Sometimes their decisions will reflect wisdom, at other times folly. With the help of our influence and support, we hope that wisdom wins out. Yet the choices, and ultimately the inherent consequences, sit squarely in the lap of each youngster.

As a high school track coach, I enjoyed working with middle-distance runners. One boy was particularly good in the 800-meter run and had qualified for the district competition. We spent a great deal of time discussing strategy, paying particular attention to determining the best pace at which he should run. At all costs we wanted to avoid being the rabbit, the runner who starts out quickly but seldom finishes.

Nevertheless, when the gun fired on the day of the race, he took off as if he'd been shot from a cannon. The first 400 meters he was well ahead of the pack. On the backstretch, however, five competitors blew by him as he finished a disappointing sixth place. Only five runners qualified for the state meet.

I had coached him conscientiously. We had worked together diligently. But I couldn't run the race for him. Even so, neither can I live my children's lives for them. I guess there is a fine line between caring enough to be actively involved and having enough faith to really let go—faith that our children will make wise decisions, and faith that when they do otherwise, they'll be able to cope with their mistake. A child's blunder does not necessarily imply a parent's failure.

Chuck Swindoll in his book, *Strengthening Your Grip* (Word, 1982), points out the fallacy of a well-accepted old adage, "Practice makes perfect." Instead, he says, practice makes *better.* I encourage you to make the most of your parent-child relationship with the realization that neither you nor your child will ever arrive at perfection. Expecting such will only result in disappointment. Relax and enjoy your children, and remember an old saying that really *is* true . . . *Nobody's perfect.*

POWER STRUGGLES

Foster Cline, a child psychiatrist, issues three rules for a happy life in his book series, *What Shall We Do with This Kid?:* (1) Avoid power struggles; (2) Pick your issues carefully; (3) Win.

What is a power struggle? If you have parented a child beyond the age of eighteen months, you've probably experienced one. It is the emotional battle of wills between parent and child. Dr. Cline suggests that power struggles tend to reduce harmony and increase tensions in relationships. For this reason, power struggles are to be avoided and the issues carefully chosen.

Some parents tend to nitpick. They criticize their child for every little behavior and misbehavior they can find. Mealtime is usually one of the primary battlegrounds. "Sit up straight. Don't talk with your mouth full. Don't chew with your mouth open. Don't sing at the table. Use the salad fork. Don't slurp your soup. Eat your peas." These and other comments are often mealtime topics of conversation.

This incessant nagging not only grates on the recipient, but also invites hostility, rebellion, and power struggles.

Oftentimes, especially in adolescence, the conversation escalates into a screaming match. While it is possible to control youngsters using our anger, this plants the seed of resentment and rarely works as the children grow older.

Think of the highway patrolman as he pulls you over to the side of the road. Does he berate you in an emotional tirade? No, quite the contrary. He civily asks for your driver's license and proceeds to deal with your traffic offense in an unemotional, business-like manner. The emotional one in this case is the driver! You see, the patrolman doesn't need to use his anger to change your behavior. The consequences speak much louder.

Remember, when confronted by angry behavior, the natural response of any person is either rebellion or insecurity, neither of which enhances a relationship. Furthermore, anger does not effectively produce the desired change in behavior.

When Carolyn was two, she became interested in the miniature potty we had made accessible in the bathroom. Within several days, she outgrew the need for diapers during the day. A few months later, we moved across town. In the stress and disruption that moving creates, Carolyn regressed considerably. She would walk into the living room, grin impishly, then proceed to wet her pants.

Needless to say, this was less than acceptable to her parents. My initial response was anger and I let her know it. The power struggle continued unabated as Carolyn completed a week of persistently irrigating the carpet. At this point I realized another approach on my part was necessary. (It only took me one week!) The next time Carolyn purposely wet her pants, I responded something like this:

Dad: "Oh, Carolyn, I see you decided to wet your pants instead of using the potty the way you used to do."

Carolyn: (She looks at me silently.)

Dad: "Do you know what that makes me think?"

Carolyn: (She shakes her head "no.")

Dad: "It makes me think that you are not getting enough sleep. You see, little babies need lots of sleep, and little babies wet their pants, too."

Carolyn: (She continues to look at me soberly.)

Dad: "Honey, when you wet your pants like a baby, I'll know you want to sleep like a baby and go back to bed. So the next time you want to go to bed, you just wet your pants, and I'll know it's time."

She tested me twice. Each time I responded very calmly as I gently carried her up to bed. I kissed her good night and let her nap in her wet pants. In two days the wetting completely stopped.

AN OUNCE OF PREVENTION

One of the best ways to deal with potentially difficult situations is to plan ahead. Those times we are caught off guard are not only frustrating, but usually handled ineffectively as well. Think about those situations that have been a source of irritation and conflict in your family. What things might be done to prevent these unpleasant occurrences?

Suppose your recent shopping trips with the children have become very troublesome. The kids are expecting souvenirs from every department. When you refuse, they fuss enough to attract the attention of shoppers three aisles away. Many youngsters find this a profitable tactic! After all, it is quite unnerving to fall under the watchful eyes of other adults.

While our initial reaction is usually to quiet the children as quickly as possible, giving in to them will only reinforce their misbehavior. We need to be confident enough as parents to do what we believe is right, regardless of what others say or think.

Nevertheless, this kind of shopping episode can be avoided entirely by simply taking preventative measures. Prior to leaving the house, gather the kids together and clearly present your plans and expectations. "Kids, we are going shopping this afternoon to buy some groceries and a birthday present for Aunt Emily. I have no intention of buying anything else. However, if you have some of your own money, you may bring it along. If you see something you like and don't have the money for it, let me know. It will give me some ideas for birthday and Christmas presents. Does everybody understand?" You might also present specific and appropriate consequences for misbehavior.

TROUBLESHOOTING

It might be wise to anticipate some other typically troublesome situations and consider how to effectively handle them. In those crucial moments, your tone of voice, motivation, and self-control will be important variables. Some parents are so busy winning the battles that they inevitably lose the peace! Our objective is to remedy a difficult situation while preserving a healthy parent-child relationship.

Turmoil during mealtime can cause indigestion and heartburn to parents and children alike. If you're like us, you rarely have a food fight; it's more often a fight about food. Here are a couple of suggestions that might help stabilize your child's eating habits.

First, allow your child one or two specific foods that he never needs to eat. After all, even adults gag at the thought of certain foods. Next, ask your children to help plan and prepare the meals. If they take part in the preparation, they are more likely to take part in the consumption. Then be realistic as to the amount of food you expect your child to consume. The average two-year-old eats much less than the typical one-year-old.

Finally, if your children do not finish their meal, they should understand there will be nothing to eat until the next meal. That means no dessert and no snacking. You might want to keep their plate in the refrigerator in case they get hungry later on—and they will.

The other night Carolyn did not finish her dinner. We didn't argue about it. We simply informed her there would be no popcorn for her at the basketball game that evening if she decided not to finish. It was very difficult for us to watch her brother and sister munching their popcorn at the game while little Carolyn had none. My heart ached for her, but she had made a choice. Sometimes it is advisable to look at the long-term benefits of situations like this rather than to pity the child. Incidentally, Carolyn didn't fuss about her loss. She knew it was her decision.

An additional thought about eating concerns snacks. If you expect your child to be hungry at mealtime, be conscious of how much you are allowing him to eat between meals.

Bedtime is another common problem for parents. An eight-year-old once told me, "My parents make me go to bed when I'm not sleepy, and wake me up when I want to sleep." Let's look at some of the issues involved in getting the children into—and out of—bed.

When it's time for bed, a child rarely responds with a bounce in his step and a song in his heart. Often he may be in the midst of an activity.

Sometimes it's helpful to simply announce that he will have to stop his activity in the next ten minutes or when he hears the buzzer on the stove. This approach allows the child ample time to complete his project and usually results in a more compliant response. Using the stove timer as a signal reduces the chances of a power struggle. After all, it's difficult to argue with a buzzer!

Bedtime, as we saw earlier, is a great time for communication with kids—if for no other reason than they want to stay up! Nevertheless, there's something special about spending the last twenty minutes of the day quietly reading or talking together. If your youngster is afraid of the dark, spend that time together in his room. This can make the room more appealing and less threatening when the lights are out.

Because young children really need routine, it helps if you give them a consistent bedtime each night. You might put them in bed at 8:00 P.M. and allow them to look at books until 8:30 P.M.

We announce bedtime at 8:00 P.M. I'll read to the children from the time they get into bed until 8:30 P.M. Therefore, the sooner they're in bed, the more time they can spend with Dad. Of course, all drinks, toothbrushing, and other bathroom functions are to be completed before they hop into bed. Any resistance after we say our prayers and kiss them goodnight at 8:30 P.M. will result in a simple choice, "Do you want to sleep with the door open or the door closed? If I hear any whining or nonsense, I'll assume you want the door closed."

If a child is school-age, getting up in the morning should be his responsibility. Buy him an alarm clock and work through the morning routine with him. Then bite your tongue, and allow him the opportunity to choose whether or not arriving at school on time is important to him. As long as you take control of his morning, he'll assume that his arrival time is your responsibility, not his.

You may want to call the school and inform them that you are working on this responsibility at home. If your child arrives late, the teacher can reinforce your efforts by making the tardiness an unpleasant experience. For most children, walking into a classroom late is enough to motivate them for many mornings to come.

You'll be surprised at how quickly your children grasp this concept if only you'll let go. Subsequently, your time together in the morning will be much more enjoyable. Your youngster doesn't like you to crab in the morning any more than you do.

Parent/teacher conference week is often a very emotional experience. The kids may be anxious about what the teacher will say, while the parent may be elated over the child's progress—or totally frustrated by the lack of it.

Sometimes in our frustration, we tend to react emotionally rather than objectively. "OK, Buddy, that's it! You go to your room and don't come out until grade cards come out again in nine weeks. We'll slide your food in under the door!"

Hey, whose grades are they anyway? Maybe the first step in dealing with grades is to help the student see that learning is his responsibility. "Boy, what a bummer it must be to get all 'F's' and one 'D.' You must be spending too much time on one subject." Or more seriously, "What a bummer it must be for you to drop from 'B's' to 'C's.' How do you feel about it? What are *you* going to do about it?"

Parents can provide structure, such as study time from 7:00 to 8:00 P.M., but punishment for unreasonable lengths of time invites resentment and does not really make the child a more motivated or responsible student.

Toys, books, and other childhood debris are often distressing to parents, but not to children. I don't think it bothers Hannah the least bit that her doll collection fills up the stairway. For her mother and I this is somewhat inconvenient, although we tolerate it for brief periods of time. Actually Ann's motto is: A home should be clean enough to be healthy and cluttered enough to be happy. If that's the basis for happiness, then our family lives in pure bliss!

In any home, some clutter is to be expected, with the understanding that it needs to be relocated from time to time. If Hannah is unwilling to pick up after herself, I will give her a choice. "Honey, are you going to pick it up and keep it in your room, or am I going to pick it up and keep it in the garage?" Another approach might be to limit the number of toys outside of the bedroom or playroom until the children have responsibly handled their clean-up duties.

Vacation trips can be stressful with a carload of youngsters. Here are some ideas for keeping the noise level down to a dull roar. Prior to the trip, put together a bag full of surprises. Then label each surprise with the recipient's name and the time for unwrapping. For instance, "To be opened by Steve at 10:00 A.M. on the second day." Coloring books, puzzles, and crafts are ideal gifts.

When the trip begins, give each child his own cake pan with a sliding cover to use as a storage container and a writing surface. With creativity and thoughtful planning, you'll reduce the likelihood of problems. You might even enjoy the ride.

HE WHO HESITATES IS LOST

There is a tendency in some homes for Mother to employ the "Wait until Daddy comes home" routine. I remember Mrs. Mondello, Larry's mom on the "Leave It to Beaver" television series, was a master at this.

If disciplinary action is in order, however, it should be handled by the parent defied, not by an uninvolved party. In addition, by the time Dad comes home, there is no relevancy to the lesson.

Some Dads, however, tend to resist even their rightful role in discipline. Why?

Many Dads spend a great deal of time away from home. When they do spend time with their children, they want it to be a very positive experience. Dads want to feel loved and accepted by their children. Somehow the thought of disciplining their children when they are so seldom together causes a great deal of anxiety. Dad doesn't want the kids to think of him as the "bad guy." Mom seems to handle things OK when he's gone, so it's very easy to make her responsible all the time.

This approach is not only unfair to Mom, but unhealthy for the children as well. Your relationship with the children will be enhanced, not hindered, by effectively taking ownership of discipline problems as they develop in your presence.

TELL IT LIKE IT IS

While it is important not to make promises you won't keep, it is equally important not to make idle threats. Children can become "parent deaf" if our words lack substance.

During a visit in another home not long ago, I watched a mother interact with her four-year-old while conversing with me. Vivacious little Rhonda sprinted through the living room. Mom reacted, "Rhonda, stop running in the house." But Rhonda never even turned her head as she scampered into the hallway. Moments later, Rhonda returned, once more whizzing right past her flustered mother. "Rhonda, I said stop that running. Any more of that and you'll get a licking." Rhonda cast an indifferent glance, then charged past her mother once more into the hallway. "Rhonda! You just wait until your father comes home."

Poor Mother was helpless—or at least she thought so. More importantly, Rhonda read Mother's apparently helpless state, too.

Fathers, if you don't mean it, don't say it. Otherwise, you'll be committed to a steady diet of crows and the haunting echoes of empty words.

Discipline in love is not only the essence of healthy rapport between Father and child, but invaluable preparation for life. It has been said that there are two lasting gifts we can give our children—one is roots, the other is wings. Establishing a balance of respect, love, and discipline early in our father/child relationship develops firmly entrenched roots. This stability lends itself to flying with enjoyment and direction rather than being blown about like a leaf in a storm.

The responsibility for these precious lives falls at our doorstep, indeed lies in our very lap. It is not merely the work of the school or the church to teach wisdom and build character. Parents, too, have the opportunity and privilege to devote themselves to the growth of their children. Biologically, you have given them life, but now you can make it special.

TAKING STOCK: DISCIPLINE

Discipline can be a difficult task. Some men react emotionally to their children's misbehavior and respond in anger on a regular basis. Other fathers prefer to make discipline a part of the mother's domain and deal with it as little as possible. There are also those dads who take an active and effective role in the disciplinary process with their children. Select which of the following numbers best describes you.

1 ____

I take an active role in disciplining my children, but it usually results in anger.

2 ____

I'm somewhere between #1 and #3.

3 ____

When I'm home, I take an active role in disciplining my children. I am confident in this role and usually handle situations effectively.

4 ____

I'm somewhere between #3 and #5.

5 ____

I expect my wife to assume most of the discipline in the family even when I'm home.

Dad's response: ______________________________

____

Ask your wife to guess which answer you selected. Then ask her to determine which one she feels best describes you. Discuss your responses in a positive and constructive way.

Wife's guess of Dad's response: ________________

____

Wife's view of Dad's position: _________________

____

Of course, #3 would be the ideal response. If your response was not #3, you may want to determine what you can do to become more active and effective in the disciplinary role. Use the space below to state your goal and plan of action. Use some of the specific principles found in the chapter.

Dad's goal: __________________________________

____

Action steps: _________________________________

____

____

____

____